"YOU SHOULD HAVE BEEN HERE YESTERDAY..."

BOOKS BY JOHN TROY

Ben: The Adventures of a Hunting Retriever (1984)

Fly Fishing! #@%&*! (1985)

Bass Fishin'! #@%&*! (1985)

Ben Again! (1986)

Fishing! #@%&*! (1986)

The Great Outdoors! #@%&*! (1987)

Ben Unleashed (1988)

Ben At Large (1990)

The Authorized Ben Treasury! (1994)

"You Should Have Been Here Yesterday . . ." (1995)

TEXT AND CARTOONS BY
John Troy

"YOU SHOULD HAVE BEEN HERE YESTERDAY . . ."

LYONS & BURFORD, PUBLISHERS

Printed in the United States of America

10 9 8 7 6 5 4 3 2 1

Design by Cindy LaBreacht

Library of Congress Cataloging-in-Publication Data

Troy, John

    You should have been here yesterday—text and cartoons by John Troy.

        p.   cm.

    ISBN 1558213600

    1. Fishing—Caricatures and cartoons. 2. American wit and humor, Pictorial.

I. Title.

NC1429.T6954A   1995

741.5'973—dc20   94-36900

                                   CIP

To Doris, my wife, my life—

and her eternal patience.

Table of Contents

1 Fishing

Fishing is the number-one participant sport in the world. Anybody can do it, and most people do. Fishermen have a reputation for absorbing punishment, not only from the elements, but also from friends and relatives and passersby.

What does a fisherman do best? He lies. About how many fish he catches and about how big they are. At least that is the average American's perception of the average fisherman.

Well, I am here to tell you otherwise. There is no more honorable group than the fishing fraternity. I know, I've been a member for fifty-one years. Those who do lie are quickly weeded out, and soon go into politics or commit a similar criminal act, do time, write books, and become millionaires.

So I'm here not to defend this quick-witted and trustworthy bunch, but to show you the lighter side of their sport. They come from all walks of life, and it's a little-known fact that the higher a person's IQ, the more that person fishes. Ask any fisherman.

When people want to relax, what do they do? They go fishing. Not tennis, not golf, not baseball. No, those are by and large games. Games are competitive. Fishing is a sport, and not competitive. That's the difference. Sports are derived from man's quest to survive. The nobility of fishing lies in our ability to exist. If you need food desperately, do you send out a golfer or basketball player? No, you send out a fisherman!

This chapter is dedicated to all those maligned and verbally abused souls who like to fish, who keep our spirits alive with the promise of catching the one that got away.

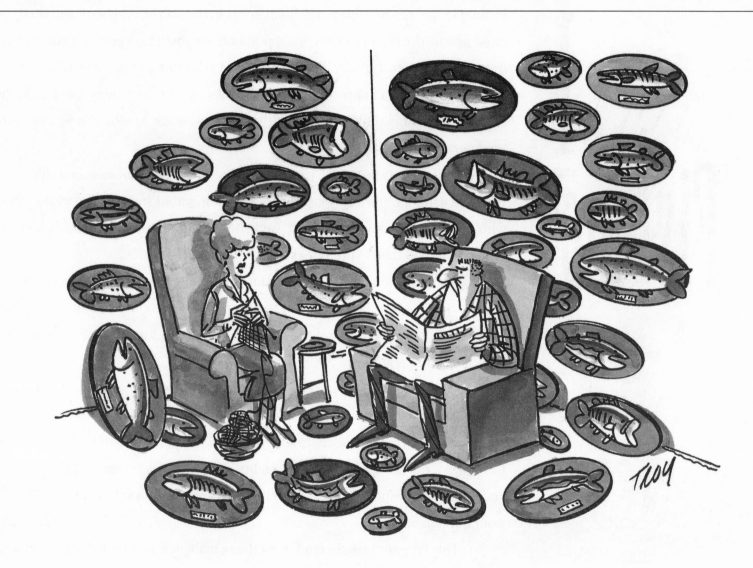

"When are you going to get caught up in this 'catch-and-release' thing?"

"... It isn't raining rain you know, it's r a i n i n g v i o l e t s ..."

"Size 14, that must be a new record for this lake!"

"Control yourself, man, it's only a few more days to trout season!"

"I still think you should have taken the fisherman out
when you used his float tube to fix the flat tire."

"Any hobbies, Mr. Jones?"

"It's a good thing our ice-fishing gear is in the *trunk*
or our day would *really* be spoiled!"

"I'm no good until I have my morning toxic waste."

"We'll look back on this someday and laugh."

"We ate it."

"I run this on peanuts."

"Look at that fishing tackle!"

"We seldom eat fish. I don't like them,
and George can't catch them."

"So . . . how long have you fished for walleyes?"

"Home is the sailor, home from the sea . . ."

"I just can't get them interested in fishing."

"*You* ask if they're biting."

"If it's all the same to you, I'll get off at the next tip-up."

"I said, 'Wind sure comes up fast on this lake!'"

"So what *is* the limit, anyway?"

"Whoops, sorry fellas!"

"These walleyes are really deep,
I must have ninety feet of line out!"

"If anybody catches that lunker, it'll probably be Herb."

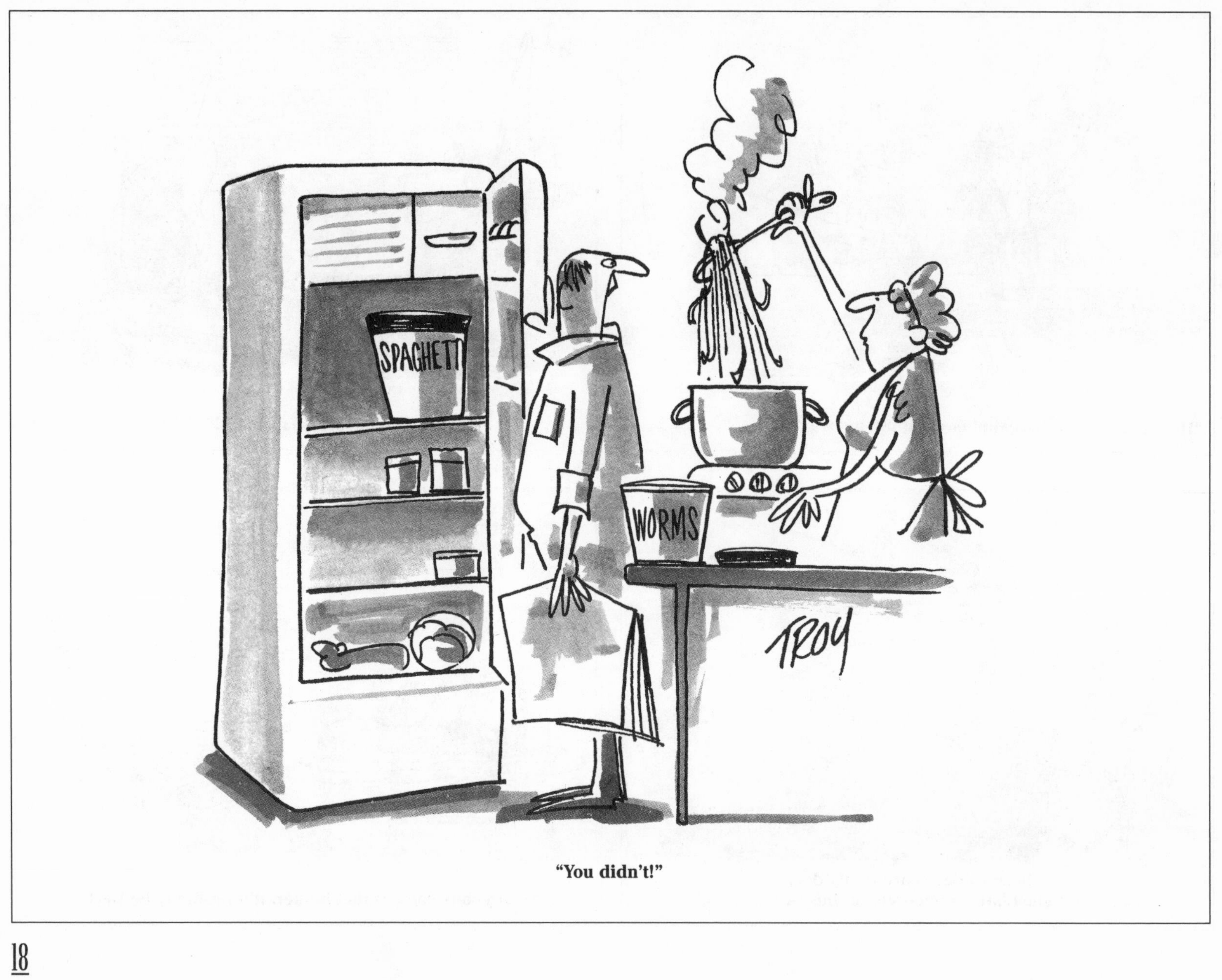
SPAGHETTI
WORMS
TROY

"You didn't!"

"He's a politician, so don't even ask him how many fish he caught."

"Must be a good place to eat. Look at all the other fishermen here."

"To tell you the truth, we haven't even seen a *sunfish*."

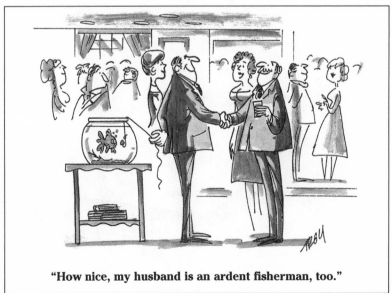

"How nice, my husband is an ardent fisherman, too."

"Ice-fishing season is never quite long enough for Edgar."

"Tell that man in the next boat he has a fish on."

"Hey, dad, tell me again about the good old days and how this stream used to teem with trout."

"You sewed a zipper on my what, dear?"

"Every day I ask myself, 'Is it worth all that misery going out in the rottenest weather to catch a few lousy little fish?' . . . and before I can answer, this idiot in me says, 'Yup.'"

"Keep a tight line!!!"

"No, no, it's take a *boy* fishing. B-O-Y . . . *BOY!*"

2
Salt Water

Only recently have freshwater anglers invaded salt water with their light equipment, even fly rods. You'll remember that years ago there was a distinct separation: You either fished fresh water or you fished salt water. Some charter boats now cater to saltwater fly fishing! Now fly fishermen and bass fishermen with slightly beefed-up tackle wander up and down our coastal beaches in search of nearshore stripers, blues, weakfish, and drum.

That anyone would consider taking saltwater fish on a fly rod was inconceivable twenty years ago, or at least wacky. Bass reels now often replace bulky saltwater reels. Some anglers even take the delicate level-winds off the bass reels to aid in winging their lures out to 300, 400, or 500 feet. Lines have gone from thick cuttyhunk to spidery monofilament of twelve-, ten-, or even six-pound test.

Novel ways to reach fish far out are being employed, from kites with snaps on them, and shooting-head fly lines, to the aforementioned bass reels.

There is no shortage of humor in saltwater and freshwater fishing, especially when you mix the two!

"This is the last time *you* plan our fishing trips."

"He gives a whole new meaning to the term '*blue*fishing.'"

"Couldn't you just show them the pictures?"

"I really prefer fresh water but heck, fishin' is fishin'!"

"Henry, don't forget to ask George about his fishing trip."

"So *that's* how he reaches offshore blues with a fly rod."

"Wow, that was one helluva cast!
Too bad your line wasn't attached to it."

3 Big-Lake Fishing

There is an element of danger and mystery to big-lake fishing. Will you hook into a big salmon, or a large football of a brown trout, or perhaps a nuclear-powered steelhead? Might even get into a big laker or northern.

Chances are about equal you'll hit a sudden squall that will test your mettle as a real fisherman, for that's when really big lake fish come alive. They love those storm fronts!

You will, too, once you've hocked your holdings for a man-size big-lake fishing boat with twin outboards and enough of that dredging equipment laughably called downriggers.

Storms come up fast on big lakes, so you'll have to invest in a powerful radio, lifesaving gear, a flare gun, running lights, a cabin for shelter—all the things a bass fisherman wishes he could afford.

This big-lake fishing gets so expensive that most guys eventually charter out their boats to pay for them, then the budget crunches or extended foul weather pops up, and zingo, there goes the boat.

But it's that element of mystery and the lure of big fish that drive the big-lake fishers. That and the necessity to go off somewhere that is inaccessible by car to lie, booze, and play cards. A last frontier, if I may.

"I can't tell if it's jumping or sounding, but it's a salmon alright!"

"Hang in there, I think he's tiring!"

"Nothing like a storm front to get those fish moving!"

"Ed's determined to high-speed troll those lakers, no matter how deep they are."

"No, no, you don't 'shot put,' just drop it over the side!"

"I think our cannonballs are bumping bottom!"

"You idiot, these are *bowling* balls!"

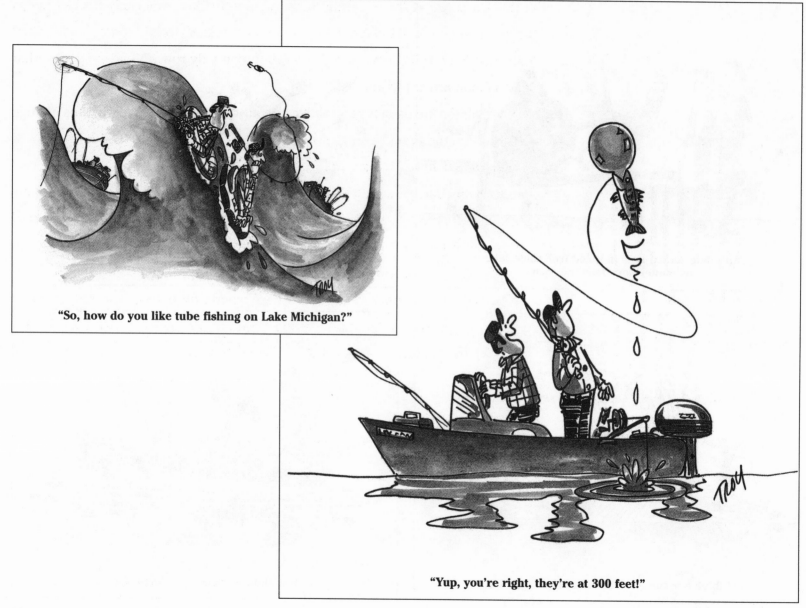

"So, how do you like tube fishing on Lake Michigan?"

"Yup, you're right, they're at 300 feet!"

4 Salmon Fishing

It takes a certain type of person to go salmon fishing, especially for twenty- to thirty-pound chinooks in the rivers of the Great Lakes. My wife calls them "crazy" persons. I've taken thirty-pound king salmon on a fly rod, and I can tell you that king salmon are not fly-rod fish!

Salmon are usually reserved for royalty, but the big spawning runs of huge salmon from the Great Lakes are within reach of us blue-collar workers. It's fun to latch onto a fish that is just itching to wrap your rod around your neck. Your reel suddenly becomes a knuckle-buster, your line a finger-burner. Your net is sometimes useless the fish are so big. Just as many nets as rods and reels are busted up on these fish. Not to mention busted knees and twisted ankles suffered in futile attempts to outrun the fish down a rocky river.

What I remember most about these wonderful behemoths is their sheer power, along with their shattering jumps that often shower you with water. Yes, you have to be a little crazy to tackle a king with a fly rod.

"You don't see many salmon runs like this one."

"So, I'm the first salmon you ever hooked on a fly, eh!"

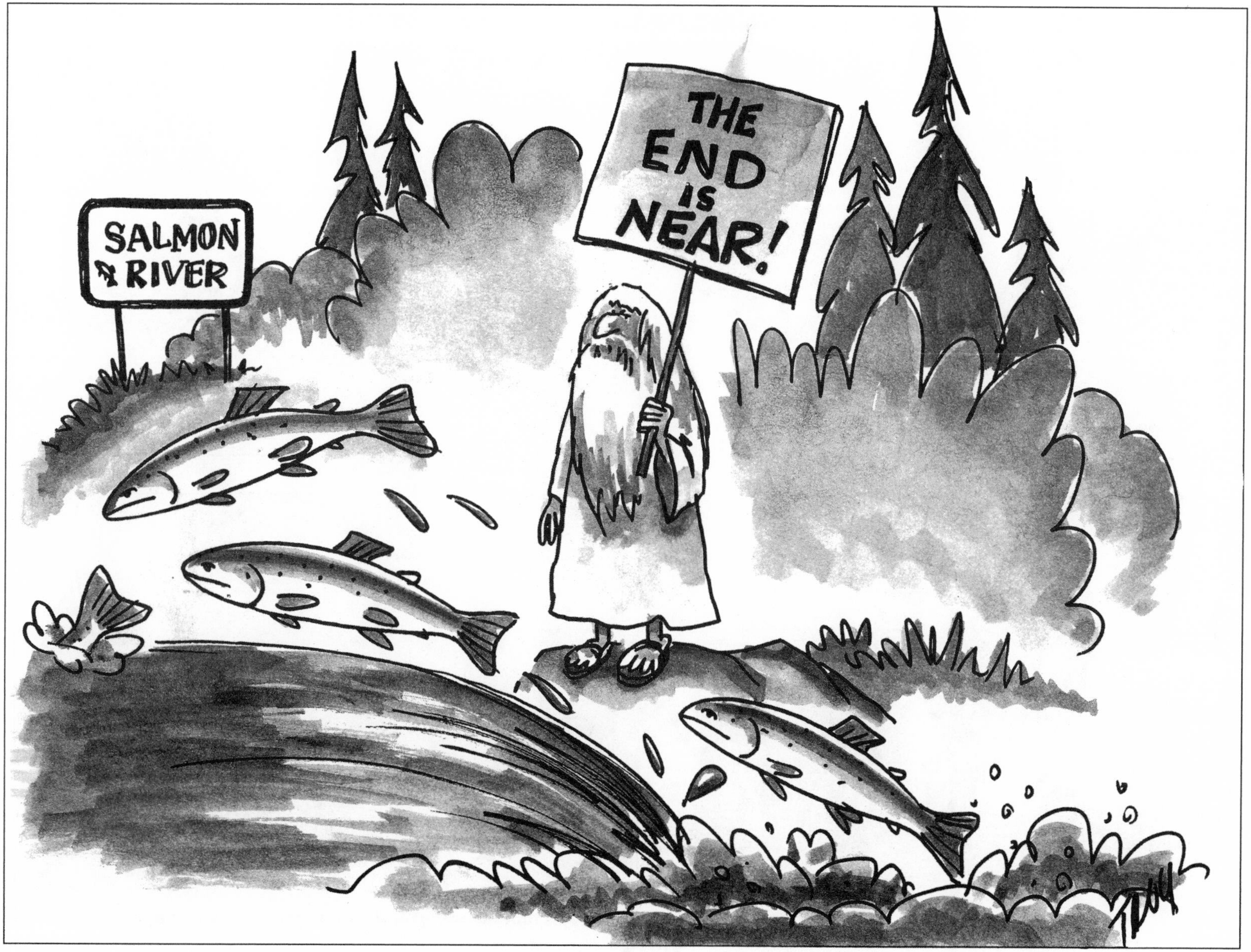
SALMON
RIVER
THE
END
IS
NEAR!

"Boy, these salmon put on quite a show, don't they?"

"No, no, you dummy, you're supposed to hit *this* fly!"

"Is that the way you get your kicks, by watching us spawn?"

"Sure like to see you hook into a big chinook with that ultralight."

"That guy thinks like a salmon."

"He said he'll land that forty-pound salmon on that 6X tippet if it takes him all day. That was last Tuesday."

5
Bass Fishing

Bass fishing has come a long way since I first cast my deer-hair mouse onto the mist-shrouded, calm-as-a-mirror waters of a northern New Jersey lake. I don't know if it's come in the right direction. Whether it's good for the bass, for the fishermen, for the manufacturers and merchandisers of bass-fishing equipment, I couldn't say. I suspect the latter. At least their efforts to elevate bass fishing to the high-tech stage have been pretty darn successful, and quite easy to poke fun at. That the modern-day bass fisherman looks more like a scientist burdened with an assortment of electronic gear and looking for something to study than a fisherman out for a day's bassing speaks well of our marketing system.

It doesn't matter that most of the lures made today are recycled copies of old favorites, as long as fishermen hit them. My tackle box is loaded with every type of lure in every color and size. Most of them will never touch water; perhaps only if it rains into my open tackle box.

There are so many soft plastic lures in my box I dare not leave it open in the summer sunlight for fear of reinventing Jell-O. That my tackle box smells like a candy factory bodes well for those whose job it is to inject every bit of plastic with an artificial fruity scent.

Antibacklash reels, reels that measure how much line is out, disengaging level-winds, adjustable magnetic drags, and so forth—the list of improvements to help us become the best angler alive is endless.

We now have 3-D sonar. No serious, up-to-date angler would leave home without one. Bass can swim, but they can't hide. Not anymore.

In the first half of this century a bass fisherman probably had two or three rods, with one being his favorite, which he used the most. Now we have pitching sticks, crankbait rods, samurai rods, crappie dusters, and dozens more.

Bass boats are homes away from home—with revolving elevated seats on platforms, steering wheels, auxiliary electric motors, gas-powered demons up to 250 horsepower or more, remote-controlled anchors—in other words, an awful lot to poke fun at.

Being a bass fisherman of sorts, I feel qualified to do just that. I hope I speak for the fish, for the bass. With the advent of catch-and-release, I hope they realize it's now just a game. We're not going to eat them. Not with any regularity, anyway, and I hope they hit my lures more, knowing this. I've been fooled hundreds of times into buying silly lures. Now I hope I can fool a few silly bass.

"Poor devil, got one of those new reels—you know, magnetic drag, left or right hand retrieve, flippin' switch, free-floating level-wind, fightin' drag, hawg handles, palming side plate . . . just couldn't handle it."

"I see you're a firm believer in the 'Large Bait-Large Fish' theory."

"Try by that old stump, there's usually a good one hiding there."

"I think your line's too heavy."

"You should have been here yesterday. They were really biting."

"Trolling? I thought you said bowling."

"I see you like doing things the old-fashioned way."

"Sure, he told me what he's using—ever hear of a woof-woof?"

"Ha, ha, fooled you, it's only plastic—say this isn't plastic at all . . ."

"I just said we'd get there first, I didn't say we'd be able to stop."

"Trolling's out of the question,
I can't do less than fifty-four miles an hour."

"You didn't see a bass boat go by here
about sixty miles an hour, did you?"

"Hey, you idiot, you made me lose a nice fish!"

"Nope, look, your scale doesn't go high enough."

"Look at this, my mouth is so big I can shove his fist right in it."

"I told you to throw it back, but noooo,
Mister Trophy Hunter wants to show everybody!"

43

"No, no, you idiot, it's plastic!"

"Don't cast too close to the shore or a darn frog will grab it.

"This is a heckuva nice fish, Bob. Put up a good fight?"

"I'll be darned—there's my sinkers, my watch, my knife . . ."

"I don't like the looks of this fish, Bobby Joe."

"No, your daddy is not going to the moon, he's going bass fishing."

"You're not going to like this, Pop, but I want to be a fly fisherman."

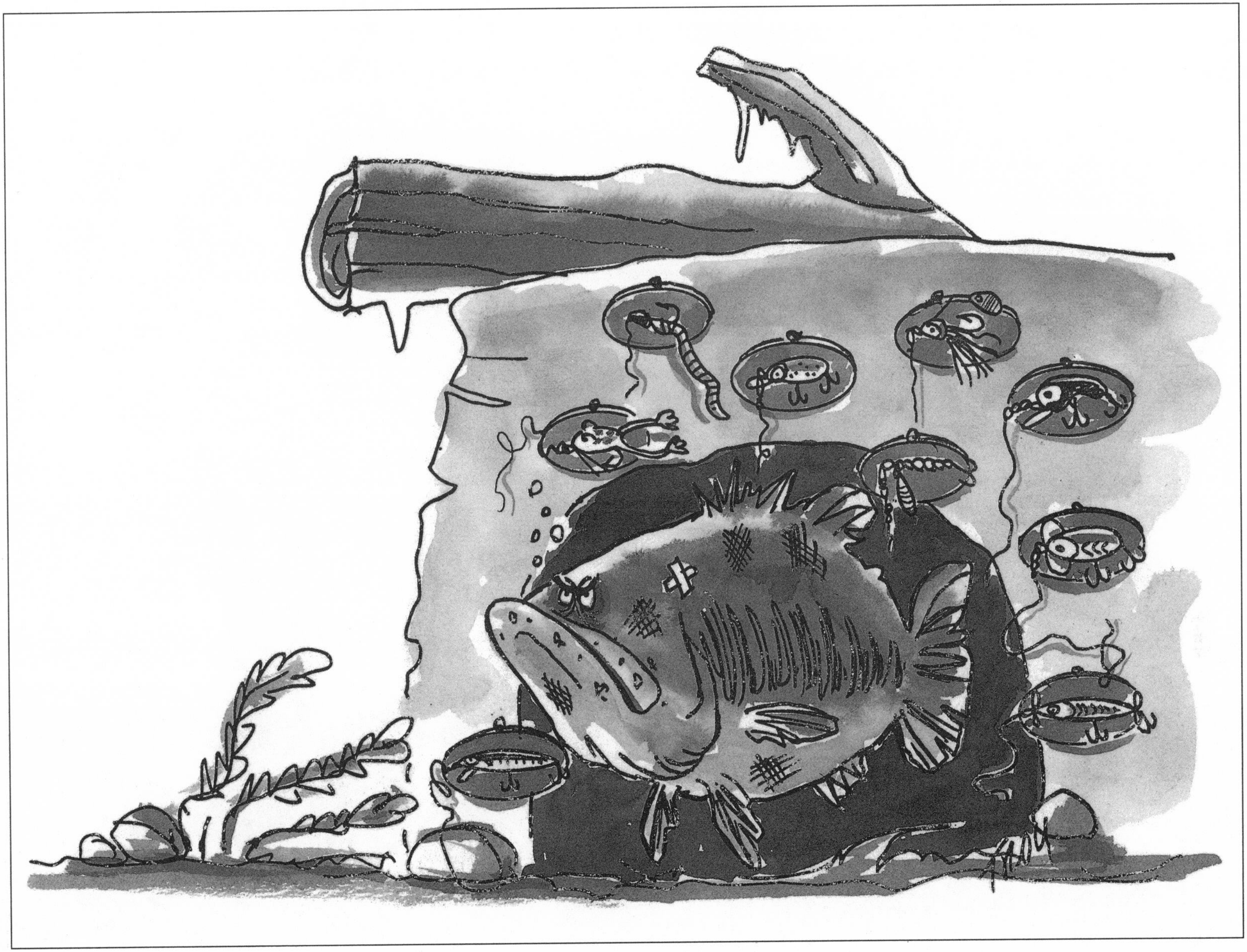

6
Muskie Fishing

"A fish of 10,000 casts" is a well-earned reputation for a noble and downright vicious fish that can grow to a scary size: the muskie! Years ago there was a movie called *The Loneliness of the Long Distance Runner*. This could well apply to the muskie fisherman: *The Loneliness of the Muskie Fisherman*.

What do you do after, say, 9,990 casts? Groan . . . Only ten more and I'll get a strike? What if I miss the strike? Do I have to cast at least 10,000 more times before I get another strike? What if I get a strike right off? Do I wait, conceivably for 19,998 more casts for another hit, assuming the next strike comes at the end of the second set of 10,000? Or with luck, might I get three strikes right away, then a gap of 29,997 casts before I get another strike? This could get tedious.

I like better the reputation muskies have earned for trollers: "One hundred miles per muskie." That's a lot of trolling. At least trolling, unlike casting, leaves your hands free to play cards, drink beer, or whittle another sure-strike muskie plug.

"When are you going to take the muskie out of the bathtub?"

"You should have seen the one I just missed!
No kidding, it must've been this big."

"So what's this I hear about you not shaving
until you catch a muskie?"

"I caught a muskie before Herb did.
Since then life has been pure hell."

"Have you ever thought of just using a nice sucker
for muskie bait?"

"I can tell you, it wasn't easy."

"Well, I've *hooked* a few muskies . . ."

"Oh good, that saves us the trouble of coming to *your* house
to see your muskie."

"You wanna talk *backbone* in a rod . . . !!?"

"Now let's see if I have this straight. You brought the muskie
up to the boat and, being an old-time bass fisherman,
you grabbed it by the lower jaw to immobilize it . . ."

"Now we're talking *muskie rod*!"

"I'd feel a lot better about catching that forty-pound muskie
if it hadn't eaten my fourteen-pound bass."

Fly-Fishing School

Some of the most popular schools going are fly-fishing schools, in which they teach fly casting, equipment selection, knot tying, and water-life identification.

Fly casting is such an art, not only pleasing to do but pleasing to watch, that it is difficult to derive humor from the act of learning it. The humor comes later, not in the teaching but when the would-be caster attempts to apply his art to wary trout or to an unwary fisherman he's hooked in a curious place.

What is taught in these schools in three days it took me years to find out on my own, and so in this case the joke is on me. But now that I teach in these schools, it is clear to me that this is a most serious aspect of fly fishing.

If there is any humor, it is that a funny thing happened to me in the fly-fishing schools, and that is I learned to fly fish all over again. And fell in love with it again.

(Thanks to Wayne Nester for this memorable quote.)

"Dad's home from his casting lesson!"

"I'm afraid that's still not quite right, Mr. Purvis."

"Hey, listen, that's not what I really meant about 'casting a fly.'"

"What makes you think fly fishing is difficult to learn?"

"As nice an 'S' cast as I've ever seen, Mr. Finlay, but I was thinking more in terms of a capital 'S,' and not necessarily in script."

8 Fly Tying

What greater thrill for a fly fisher than to catch a trout or salmon on a fly that he or she has tied? Unless it is after he or she has tied that first fly and it stays on the hook.

There are schools that teach you how to tie flies, or you can learn it from books, or from a fly-tying friend.

There is no doubt fly tying is an art, but I've often thought that if my dog had opposable thumbs she could master this art. Not to say it is easily learned, for there are some 1,700 patterns, and variations by the dozen of each pattern. Anything over a dozen leaves me out of the race, anyway.

Why would anyone, you ask, want to spend so much time and effort tying up dozens of flies when they cost only a buck and a half each? This is a case where the question becomes the answer. The average fly fisher loses about a hundred flies a year to snags, fish, trees, and gusts of wind, gives some away or loses a fly box, any one of a hundred reasons. It costs about a quarter to tie one of your own.

This is another area of fishing where women do better, due to their earlier training in sewing class. We men, meanwhile, spent our formative years slamming our heads together in what we like to call "contact sports." Not easy to tie up a #24 Trico spinner with that constant ringing in our ears and a balanced number of dead cells helping us to concentrate. Me, I'm still trying to figure out how my newly acquired whip-finisher works.

"What's this I hear about you coming up with
a revolutionary neck hackle?"

Matching the hatch.

"Ow, hey!"

"Aren't you overdoing this roadkill thing a bit?"

"So who taught you how to tie flies?"

"Is that a parachute fly?"

"Ah, there's a productive pattern!"

"There, there, I was all thumbs when I first started, too."

9 Fly Fishing

Fly fishing has taken unprecedented steps and directions in the last decade or two. It is now a blue-collar sport. It's not exclusively so, but most members of the clan *are* electricians, carpenters, realtors, or insurance salesmen—the craftsmen who keep our country ticking.

Since I am one of these craftsmen (yes, cartooning is a craft), it is my God-given duty to pass the word that fly fishing is the highest form of fishing. But in doing so it's necessary to puncture the pomposity of those who, until now, have controlled the sport. Elitism is on the way out, but it's not dying easily. One of the problems is that as soon as used-car salesmen, for example, take up the long rod, they begin to feel elevated, different, better, *above* other fishermen. They become elitists! So I try to key in on the pomposity and the elitism of the sport.

Now, at least on the stream, the fly-fishing carpenter is better than any CEO who uses spinning gear, or any high-profile politician who wanders onto a waterway with a casting rod and worms.

Those who use worms are scorned by fly fishers. Those who fish with corn kernels are silently berated. Salmon eggers, too. Yet almost every fly fisher begins as a wormer, an egger, or a yank-and-crank spin fisher.

Like the guy who is of twenty-seven nationalities and can tell ethnic jokes without threat of physical retribution, I confidently hammer away at the elitist side of fly fishing. Maybe it's because I began as a wormer, or at least as a Japanese beetler catching sunfish with a cane pole at the age of four. In a sense I am poking fun at myself. It's easy to do. Just ask my friends.

But underneath all this I love *all* fisherpeople. They are kindred spirits, and I am happy to be among them. And I hope they accept this humor as it is intended, so we can laugh at ourselves.

"It was her late husband's most prized possession
and she wouldn't part with it, so I bought the old lady, too."

"I used to have a boron rod, but the bank repossessed it."

"I spent half my life searching for the perfect rod.
Finally I said the heck with it."

"Are you kidding, this new custom-made bamboo rod
doesn't go *near* the river!"

"You would never know it, but I haven't used a fly rod in years."

"You certainly had a nice cast going there, young man."

"Your fly snapped off an hour ago, young man,
but you were casting so beautifully I didn't want to disturb you."

"Relax, Ed, you're too tense."

"Use the green one . . . they won't rise today . . .
try that number 18 . . . make sure your leader sinks:
Do you think you know everything!"

"Pardon me, I couldn't help but notice your rod is falling below
the one o'clock position during the backcast, your wrist is not
straight, and you're dropping the rod tip too early on the forward
cast, which can result in not only wind knots, but also—say,
you don't mind my telling you this, do you?"

"There's a lunker trout that lives in this pool,
but nobody seems able to outsmart him."

"I have this recurring nightmare of myself fishing the Firehole and making a magnificently long cast, my dry fly cocking beautifully to begin a drag-free float on the emerald green water. Every fisherman up and down the river begins applauding me. Then the *fly sinks* . . . and a trout *grabs it*!"

"I notice you're using a sinking line."

"We're back. So how was your winter?"

"I'll bet you can't wait for trout season."

"I figured, heck, why stick him in a kennel
when hunting season ended."

"Fly fishermen are a different breed, alright."

"Cold front snuck right up on that city feller."

"Okay, the first @*!#&* that says 'How are they biting?' is a dead man!"

"Whatever you do, don't ask him if he foul-hooked a carp and for two hours thought it was a salmon."

"Hey, sorry, I thought it was a bug."

"Does it surprise you that I've read Hemingway's *Old Man and the Sea* and Melville's *Moby Dick*? After all, I *am* a wise old brown trout."

"Here, need some insect repellent?'

"Do you think that, somehow, they *know*?"

"I've taught you everything I know about fly fishing, now if only there was some way you could hold the rod."

"This is a good idea as long as we don't run into a three-hundred-pound brown trout."

"I know these trout are hard to sneak up on, but this is ridiculous."

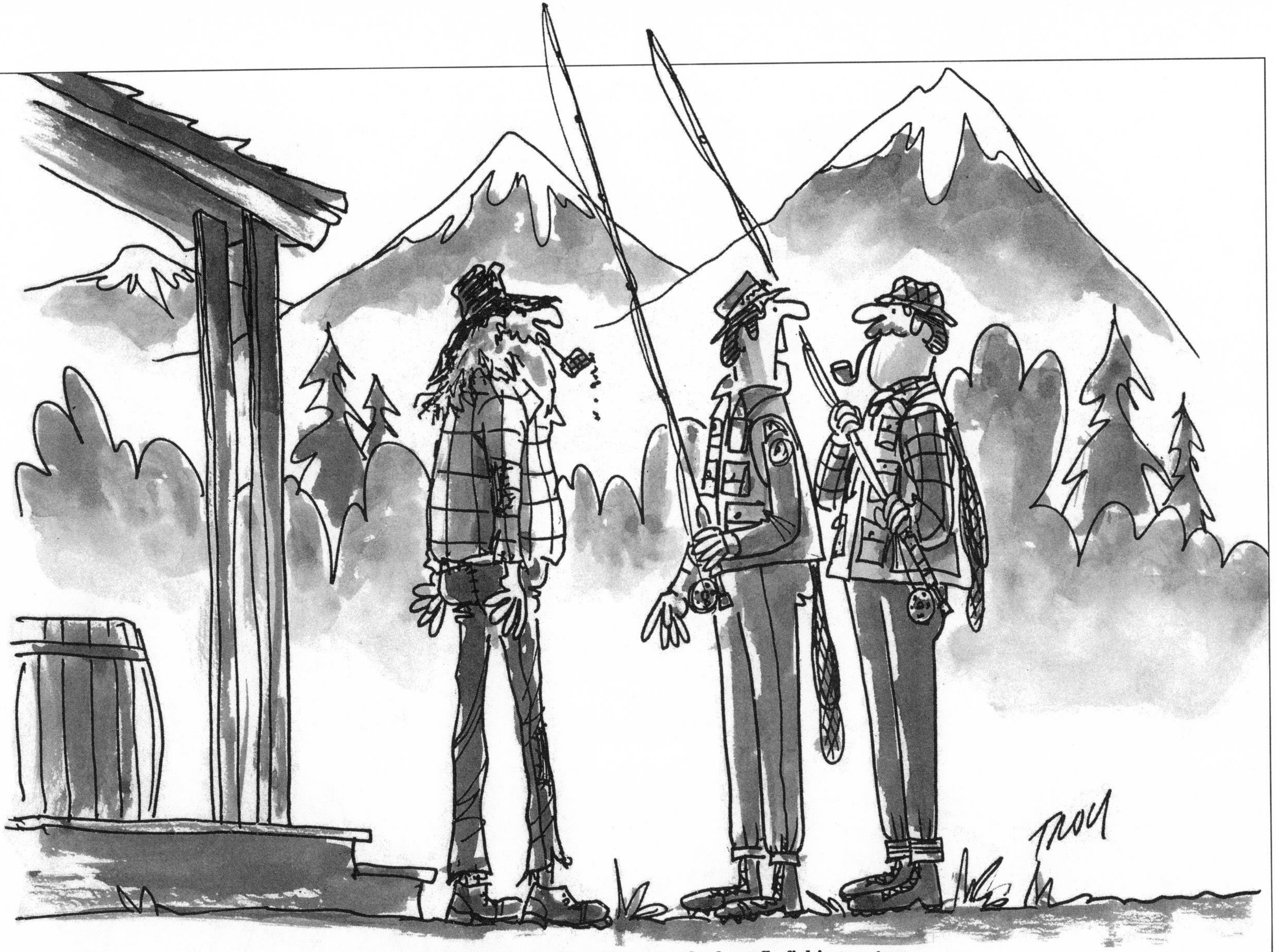
TROY

"He says, hell, yes, he'll guide us to the best fly-fishing waters
in these mountains, but first he wants to know what these long wavy sticks are."

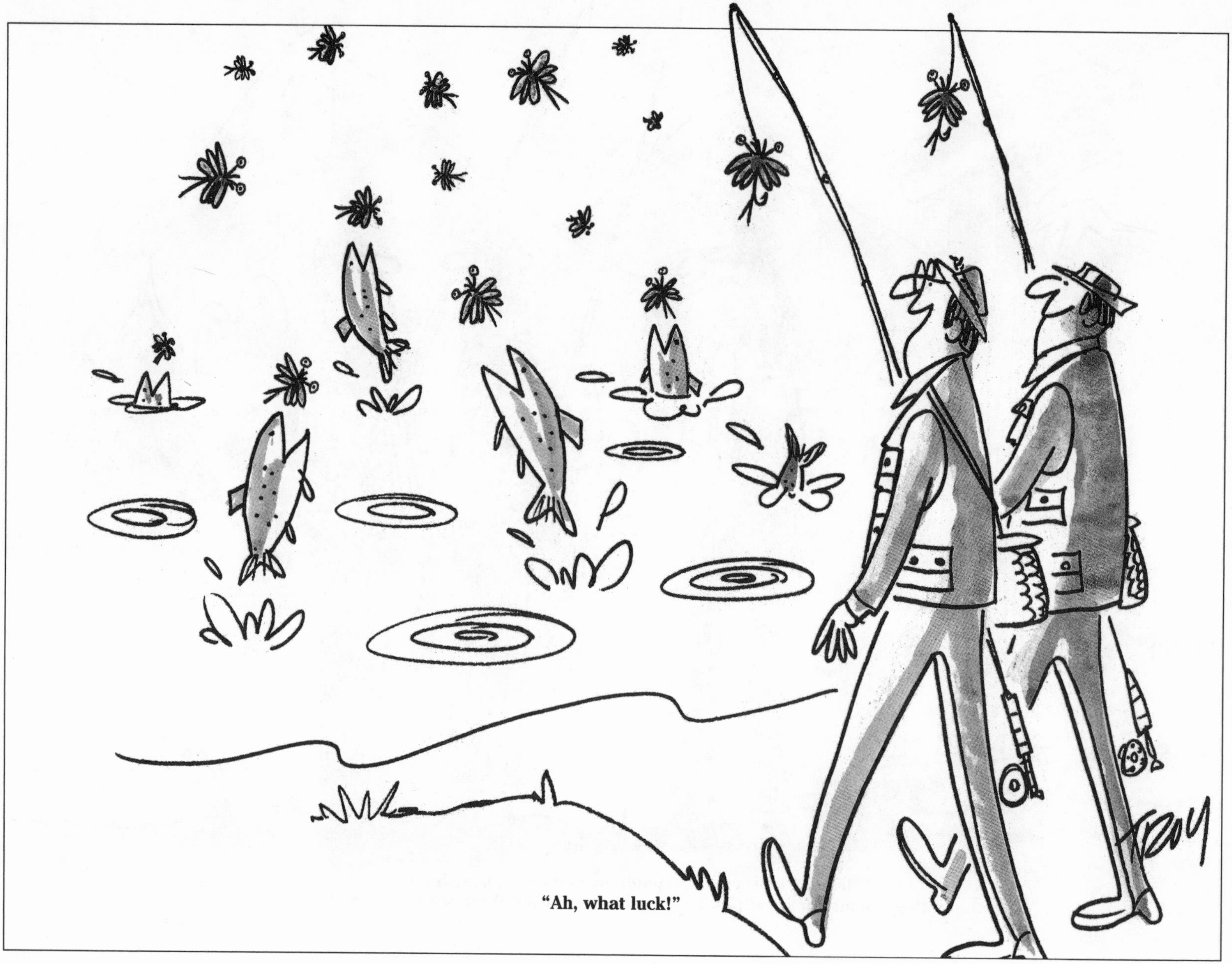
TROY

"Ah, what luck!"

"Never mind me, which fly are they rising to?!"

"You don't see many rises like *this* one."

"George's belief is that all fish should be released to be caught another time. Someday he's going to catch one, to justify his philosophy."

NO-KILL WATERS

ALL FISH MUST BE RETURNED TO THE

"Excuse me, I couldn't help noticing that you're fly fishing."

"For the love of God, man, switch to wets . . . they'll never rise in seas like this!"

"Say, I'm kind of new at this.
How do you keep these flies on the hook?"

"Does this stream have a slippery bottom?"

"I was a flower child in San Francisco—man,
then I discovered fly fishing!"

"Control yourself, Peasely, when they don't hit on flies, *they don't hit on flies—it's all part of the game!*"

"You want a real fish taker? Garden hackle, that's what!"

"To give you an idea how bad it's been, *that* is a feeding frenzy."

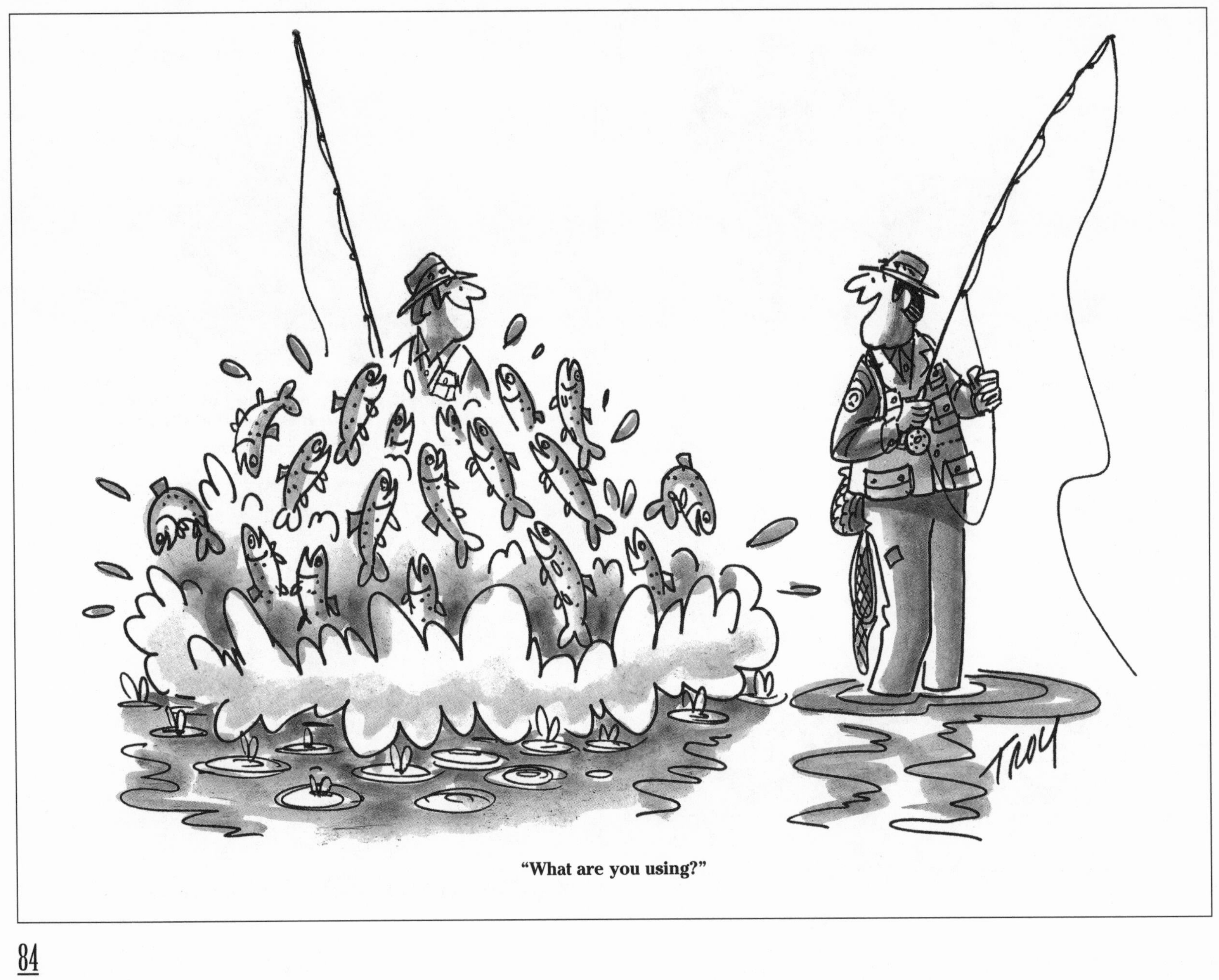
TROY

"What are you using?"

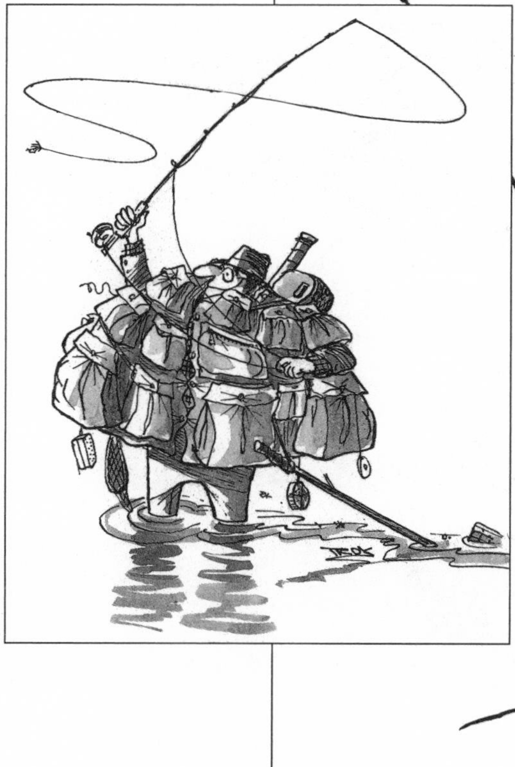

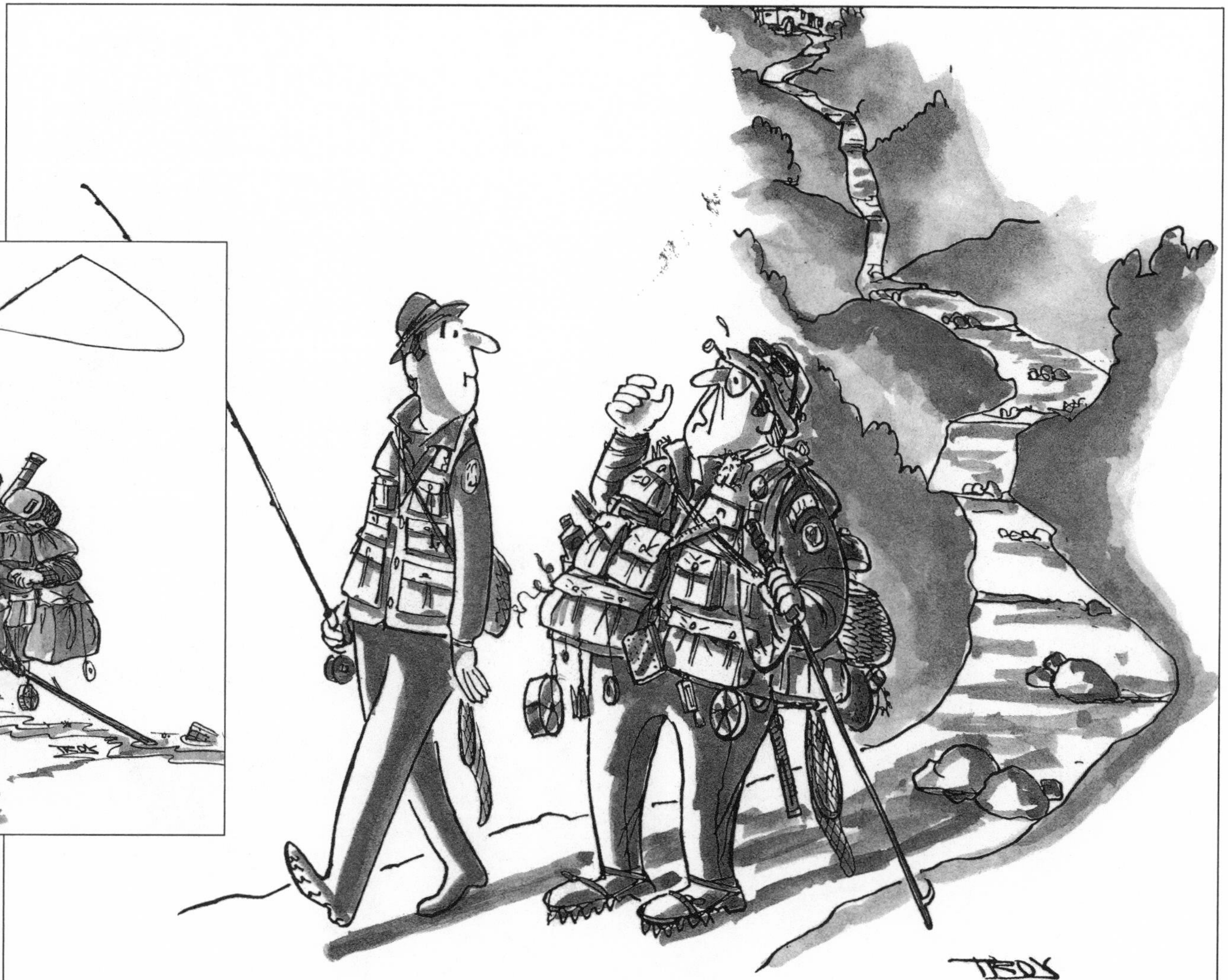

“I forgot my fly rod.”

"I am honored to be your guest speaker . . ."

"H E Y!"

"Something tells me dry flies won't do the job today."

"Are you using wets or dries?"

"Well, *sure*, if they're jumping I use dry flies, too."

"He's strictly wet flies."

"I'll have a Ginger Quill, and make it extra dry, please."

"I've been admiring your casting,
but your choice of flies leaves a lot to be desired."

"C'mon, lighten up and troll the right way."

"Every chance I get, I'm outta that office."

"You'll never know how much George has been looking forward to your party."

"Waiter, there's a *Musca domestica* in my soup."

"Quick, hit that pocket over there with your Muddler!"

"My husband is preparing himself for Opening Day."

10
Snaggers

I have a special place in my heart for snaggers. In my younger years we used to snag suckers. Let's be honest, we snagged almost everything. Things were different then, but our code of ethics wouldn't let us snag trout or bass, especially spawning bass.

Salmon snagging was rampant from the 1960s to the late 1980s, but now it is illegal in most states. Your typical snagger was the guy next door, if the guy next door was a second-grade dropout. But if you needed a salmon on the table, you sent out a snagger. Why send a boy out to do a snagger's job?

The snaggers I've drawn don't look like real snaggers (remember, I was a snagger) but look the way we *think* snaggers should look. One of them did look that way, however, and I like the fact that *that* individual ran up the middle of the river one December day to try to snatch a muskrat off a log. That he ran in front of us to spoil our fishing, and the fact that his waders were split up the back and water was pouring in and out earned him the right to serve as my model. I hope he appreciates this, and I hope I never see him again.

"Pardon me, would you suggest a 2X or 4X tippet for these salmon?"

"C'mon your Honor, do *I look* like the kind of guy
that would *snag a salmon*?"

"Snagging? Are you kidding? Look, there's a worm on my hook,
a salmon egg, a minnow . . ."

"What do you mean, 'swallow the evidence?'"

"Last night I watched Hemingway's *The Old Man and the Sea*. Sure makes you proud to be a fisherman, don't it?"

11 Women

Women have always fished, but men, being inherently lazier, kind of took over the sport. Fishing is better than housework, or any work. Work is for people who don't know how to fish. Fishing, then, is for people who don't know how to work.

Women are society's workers. Check out any society, past or present. Guys were always going off somewhere and fooling around, while women kept things going at home.

It stands to reason, then, that when women began to fish seriously, they did it better than men. They work harder at it. But with fishing being structured along patriarchal lines it's only recently that women, as a group, have come to the fore. It's not that we men, as a group, didn't try to keep them down. No, but cream always rises to the top, class tells, and so we find more and more women in our sport, making us look silly. We always were, but now we're being noticed.

The invasion has begun, and by 2020 or thereabouts we'll find pretty nearly equal numbers of men and women out fishing. All we have to do now is teach them how to lie, drink heavily, and avoid work every time it rears its ugly head.

P. S. W O M E N by John's Wife!

Women have always been fishing. First it's with their dads, where they learn the basics, then with their boyfriends, where they get more experience in the diversity of the sport. Just when they are becoming more and more expert something happens: marriage and family! Notice how when these things occur it is always the women who give up *their* sports. Well maybe today it's different, but back in time women were expected to change *their* whole lifestyles and assume most of the responsibilities of home and family. The men still went fishing and hunting.

So by the time women fish again, they are rusty, and have to refresh their memories and fine-tune their skills to pick up where they left off with their sport. The men have, meanwhile, become more experienced and expert at their sport.

Times are changing . . . before the year 2020 . . . ?

"If I didn't love you, would I take you trout fishing?"

"She likes to go with me, but really doesn't care that much for fishing."

"This may be your idea of a fish fry, but it certainly isn't mine!"

"May I have a new fly? This one is all messed up."

"Will it really help our relationship if I throw it back?"

"Must you punctuate each fish you catch with 'Score one more for the ERA!?'"

"I don't really care that you tie flies better than me, or that you can cast farther, or even that you catch more fish than I do. What gets me is that you look so damned good doing it!"

"But isn't the fly supposed to land on the water now and then?"

12
The Perfect Rod

As a young man I recall struggling with rods that were too "soft" or too "stiff"—the idea being that "soft" rods cast wet flies well, and that "stiff" rods cast dry flies well. Hence, "wet-fly-action" rods and "dry-fly-action" rods. A noble concept, but flawed. Since these notions have been dispelled during the last thirty years, we now can claim to understand the dynamics of fly casting, and, through a complicated series of upper body gymnastics, apply these principles to the creation of the perfect rod!

Just as each civilization has its own god—perfect, nonetheless—each rod maker claims to have the *right* god, er, rod for you, ranging from teeny three-footers (anything shorter than that I refuse to discuss) to willowy, feathery twelve-footers (anything longer than that the telephone company can discuss) that can lay out lines almost vertically.

We are surprised to find that many different rod companies buy "sticks" (bare rod shafts) from a single manufacturer, then with some swift magic—magic eyes, magic wrappings, magic finish, magic ferrules, and such—fashion rods that are far superior to their competitors' magic rods. Where, you ask, do they get this "magic" stuff that makes their rods the best? "We," they say, "get it from . . . God." Okay, they don't say *that*, but they might just as well.

If these rods *are* so perfect, or even slightly magical, how come we (may I speak for you, too?) have such problems casting with them? Is it our fault—each man kills the thing he loves, including a perfect fly rod—or is it the rodmakers'? Or is it human error, that ethereal culprit who downs 727s and overheats nuclear domes? It's not nice to know there is, in the whole world (including Taiwan and Korea) only one *perfect* rod *exactly* suited to *your* needs, one that balances with you *perfectly*. It's not easy to find this elusive wand, or economical.

But if "the struggle is the thing," maybe it's just as well we search on, getting out on the rivers and streams, keeping us attuned to nature, and out of trouble.

"Spaghetti" rods and "war clubs" were the main fare forty years ago (unless you wanted to trade in your house or new car for one of the kingly custom-made jobs) and we soon learned that balancing rod to reel to line to leader to fly to ourselves wasn't easy. As the man walking through a barnyard soon learned, we had to adjust our stride, to be able to set our own pace with each individual rod. We learned to cast slowly with "soft" rods and fast with "quick" rods, to play fish with "soft" rods and horse them in with "stiff" rods. Yes, we learned to watch our step.

The weight of a fly line determines which rod to get. Even years ago we knew we should choose the line first and leave it to the rodmaker to provide a superb rod for the line. (The real truth, or perhaps a gut tendency, was to buy the rod first, since it was the more expensive item. Or we were forced to buy a line for a rod we'd gotten for Christmas or at a sale.) This often led to overloaded rods, because the tendency was (and still is) toward lines that are too heavy: "Hey, are you kidding, buster, I got a powerful wrist! Of course I can handle a 10-weight lead-core torpedo taper!" So we spent most of the fishing day trying to pry the line off the water's surface.

Just as bad is a line that's too light, one that won't turn over, a line that doesn't bring out the rod's *action*. I like that term. A rod's *action*! "Your line doesn't bring out the action in your rod," the experts warn. "The line doesn't *speak* to your rod!" A more intellectual warning.

Lines that are too light also tend to flip upward at the slightest urging from the rod, then fall in a floppy, noodly mess at our feet. It's almost as if the *power* in your rod is saying to the line: "There, take *that*, you *wimp*!"

About this time we were seeing the last of the "limpo" rods and "telephone poles." I liked the telephone poles. Mine was, and is, a Granger Aristocrat, a nine-foot, six-inch rod weighing five and three-quarters ounces. If ever there was a reason to take up bait casting or spinning, this rod was it. A typical day on a bass lake would find me casting the fly rod for five minutes with a deer-hair mouse, then using a spinning rod for the next hour to rest up. Even a bluegill on the Granger felt like a lunker. After a while I'd get the feeling

that bluegills *invented* leverage. As I grew up and my body weight surpassed 135 pounds, I became very fond of the rod and adjusted to it—you know, cast out a hummingbird-size hair bug, let it lie still for twenty minutes (yes, really big bass *do* hit motionless lures), cast again, wait twenty minutes more—a very restful day afloat, I must say.

In bear country, salmon fishermen still love this type of rod: "Hey, there's a bear after my salmon!" "Okay, hit him with your rod." POW! Better than a .357 magnum.

104

Meanwhile, glass rods had been refined into very adequate, but not perfect, fishing tools. Alas, the search was still on.

Graphite rods soon followed. Lighter, quicker, and *more expensive* than glass rods, these glamour sticks can lay out impressively long casts, "kicking out" line for almost unbelievable distances. They can also shatter sometimes, with a sound that can be heard around your budget for months. Tap one too hard in just the right way and you'll have two midge rods—one "soft," the other "stiff." Just like that. This makes fly fishing second only to polo as a rich man's sport. But there was an answer to this problem.

That answer was, and is, the composite rod. (Did I overlook boron? Or is boron just a fancy kind of graphite?) Composite rods are just that, composites of graphite, boron, fiberglass resins, magic glues, and such. And don't forget magic single-foot line guides, bonded wrappings, flex ferrules . . . Oh, I can hardly stand this! Before they got it right, however, we got some funny rods that flexed in odd places. To get around this, some rod builders began calling these creations (I like to call them Frankenstein babies) "slow" rods and "fast" rods. They really did. Sound familiar?

Slow rods flex all the way down by your casting hand, while fast rods bend only at the very end, between the tip-top and the first guide. (They had the same trouble with steel rods early in this century, then with solid glass, with hollow glass, and with graphite rods too, but by this time you would think *some* of the dynamics would be harnessed, wouldn't you?) Anyway, to make a long story short . . . and that's just the way rod builders went!

Short! Yes, we learned that shorter meant better. Or at least sportier. Brush rods, flea rods, midge rods—all those words that get you scratching. I got one. Not an itch, a rod that is. Because it was "sporting." About as sporting as playing the bongos up a brick wall. While these rods are great for short work, any cast longer than forty feet concerns itself with the process of whipping the rod back and forth so smartly that the helicopter effect is enough to lift you right out of the water. And tiring! Just try walking around for a few hours with your arm up, bent at the elbow, karate-chopping the air at the rate of seven chops a second and you'll have a fair idea of what I mean. They should be called aerobic rods.

Remember the old saying: "That's the long and short of it!" Well, here's the long of it, for recently very long rods have been popping up—rods up to ten, eleven, and even twelve feet long. Now we can easily lift our line, leader, and fly from eight or nine feet over the ground to God knows where, up above riverbanks, treetops, and silos. But how do we bring the blessed fly down, especially when the trout are rising scant feet in front of us? What do you do with seventy feet of curls, spirals, S-loops, and figure eights drifting merrily about high in the clouds? Well, you have the parachute cast, which consists of nothing more than dropping your line on the water in a series of curls, spirals, and figure eights. This creates another problem, namely what to do with all that mess should a trout take the fly. Luckily, any rod that can propel a line seventy feet vertically should, with a quick snap of the wrist, quickly straighten out the whole affair and set the hook. But how do you play a trout six feet away on seventy feet of line? About now an eight and one-half or nine-footer handling a 6- or 7-weight line is beginning to look mighty good to you, right?

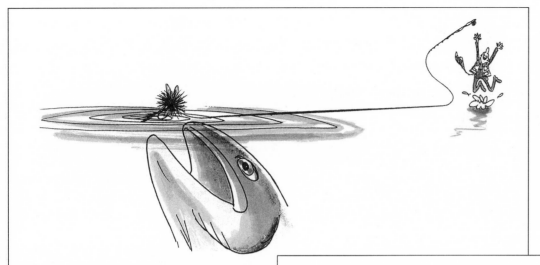

Somewhere along the way, despite all these conspiracies against us, we begin to get off some pretty fair casts. Then, one clear autumn day after a full summer of practice, we lay out a beauty, a real gem! We leap into the air with great joy, exhilarated! Unfortunately our rapture outweighs our prudence. We drop the fly rod. A cutthroat grabs the superbly cocked Coachman on the end of our exquisitely straight leader, then heads downriver to the sea, jerking our new composite graphite along with him.

But if we live long enough and have the necessary gall and recuperative powers to practice this most demanding of all arts, we soon manage back-to-back fine casts. Then, perhaps a week later, a string of three or four, interspersed, of course, with some horrible snarls, hooked ears, broken tips, snapped leaders, and such. We have now found our elusive perfect rod! Hallelujah, our *precise matching outfit*! Not only does it match itself, it matches *us,* too! We venture forth for a day's trouting filled with new confidence.

Does the sun really shine brighter lately? Are the trout taking our flies with greater gusto? Are our casts actually *nice*? Or, after this long struggle, are we a mite punchy? Did it take too long, are we getting a little senile? A friend told me recently: "At long last I've learned to appreciate my casting ability." "How's that?" I asked. "I lowered my standards," he answered.

I imagine that's the way to find the perfect rod, too.

13
What Fishermen Eat

Sometimes a fisherman is determined to live off what he catches. Here we find one of these sports with a large spotted water newt, his day's catch . . . and his evening's meal.

How to sneak by a bull? Easy. Just eat grass, Pretend to be grazing. Try to look like a cow. If the look on the bull's face turns from one of indifference to one of lust, you have been *too* successful. Proceed to set a world mark for the 400-meter run, or head for the nearest fence.
A lot depends on it.

Brookies are tasty, but small. Check your compendium for the number you're allowed to keep. Take your limit . . . plus a powdered protein supplement. Maybe a couple of hamburgers and a can of beans will fill out your meal.

Eat what the guide eats, even if you don't know what it is, or if it moves sporadically. Don't insult him by refusing his offering. Your fish take may fall off dramatically, may perhaps even conform to Sierra Club standards.

The "wishful thinking" dietary plan. The "light of your life" finally goes fishing with you. She insists you sample her chocolate-covered bees. You find out the chocolate is okay. However, from that day on every time you see a McGinty bee in fly-tackle catalogs, you retch visibly.

A misprint in the beginners' fly-fishing manual said "set to cook" rather than "set the hook," which would have made no difference to our trout-chasing friend. He loves panfried trout so much he'd just as soon forget the preliminaries.

III

It's usually a good idea to steam-clean your creel at the start of the season. And never carry liverwurst sandwiches around all day in the hot sun. But, like the guy who always gets a seat on the bus because he loves garlic, this may be the answer to having lots of elbow room on your favorite fly stretch.

Talk about your fresh-caught fish!

After a long, long winter, the Baetis hatch finally begins. A small number of heretofore supremely patient dry-fly fishers in the local stream crack, and begin to go on a feeding frenzy.

It's universally known that next to catching trout a fisherman most loves to eat trout. Any expertise concerning trout, unfortunately, is often left at streamside, or at the tying vise. Rarely if ever does it encompass the good ol' cookout—trout fry, if you will. The offerings at the outdoor grill are another case of cookbook misprint—parboil being read as *char*broil. Eat heartily, anyway, or you'll never be invited back. Lucky you! Go fishing instead.

Conversely, we find there are many things, millions upon millions in fact, that eat fishermen—black flies, mosquitoes, no-see-ums, snakes, crocs, etc.—thus supporting the "food chain theory" in which the strong prey upon the weak, the large upon the small, and the intelligent upon the less intelligent.

No fly fisher worthy of the title would think of keeping—much less eating—any of those precious few native brookies. They'll often go to great lengths to dine only on hatchery-reared trout. Not to mention great expense.

14
What Fishermen Are Afraid Of

Ah, fishing, the most pleasant of all pastimes. Troubles and fears tumble off downstream, lost amid the gurgling sound of a sparkling mountain stream. The voice of serenity whispers through tall pines—here is a man at peace as he casts over pristine waters to rising speckled beauties. But wait! Did a frown, like the shadow of a flitting bird, just cross his brow? What could cause that in this cathedral of contentment? A closer look finds him muttering under his breath, his eyes flitting nervously from bank to bank. What is he looking for? Is he . . . afraid of something? Not here! Not on a trout stream! But yes, and if you're a fisherman, you know the cause of his anxiety, that nervous tic on his brow, because you, too, know *what fisherman are afraid of.*

Swimmers. The fear here is that you'll foul hook one of these misguided folk. But after being hooked once or twice, most of them have learned not to go swimming where somebody's fishing. This makes a case, too, for barbless hooks. It makes the learning process quicker, and less painful for all involved.

Bugs. Of course, bugs . . . no-see-ums, mosquitoes, deerflies, horseflies, ticks, and any number of tiny blood seekers. Some efforts to protect against the hordes of pests are fruitless, some downright ingenious, some impractical. Do your fishing in December. So what, no fish—no bugs either.

Crowds. It may seem like a street gang has descended on your favorite trout stretch. Don't sweat it. Go home for a couple of hours. They'll destroy each other. The only evidence of combat will be some broken bottles, worm cans, a ripped hip boot . . . .
Pick up the litter, drop it in a trash can, and enjoy your solitary fishing. You've learned an important lesson—don't fish for at least six hours after the stocking truck has left.

Slippery rocks. You've heard of football knee. Well, an even greater medical problem (at least to anglers) is "fishing knees," caused by slipping on and slamming down onto slippery rocks. Many stream bottoms develop a coating of what can only be called "brown, oily catsup." Is the streambed made up of walnut-size, baseball-size, grapefruit-size, or football-size rocks with an occasional living-room-size boulder thrown in? It's important to know this, for there are many fine solutions: wading shoes, felt soles, creepers, rock grippers, even strap-on items that can only be described as economy-size ice tongs. Each fits a certain size rock. But the real trick is to wade as though you are walking through a cow pasture—walk between the things.

Speaking of cows, fishermen do their best to avoid bulls. It's helpful to know the difference between a cow and a bull. Skulking past a cow is not only bush-league stuff, but could set you up for a real letdown, especially if a bull is skulking up on you.

Waders full of water can be fun, annoying, or deadly, depending on whether the water is eighty degrees, sixty-five degrees, or thirty-two degrees, and whether you are half zonked, seriously fishing, or trying to commit suicide. Go home and dry out (both ways if you're half zonked). Be careful of hypothermia.

My uncle always interpreted NO TRESPASSING signs to read "WELCOME SPORTSMEN, ONE AND ALL." The real trick, he would say, is knowing sign language. If the message "no hunting" was in big letters and "or fishing" in small letters just below, the poster was really put up to keep hunters out. Fishermen were, well, okay. If the poster said NO HUNTING, FISHING, BERRY PICKING, he'd say: "Hell, I ain't doing *all* those things, *I'm only fishing*!" And fish he would. A bottle of whiskey or a box of candy would go to the irate landowner pushing his or her point. It really worked.

Dry spells are a real fear, especially to the trout. The trickle that used to be a stream calls for accurate casting over very spooky fish. If you wish to succeed on low water, first practice casting into a saucer forty feet away on your lawn. If you can't hit the saucer at least one out of five casts, resort to pond fishing for bass until the fall rains come. Ponds are easier to hit. Or bring that bimbo along who brags of seventy-five-foot of casts into a tea cup, and watch him miss the trickle of a stream time and again. Hey, it's been a rough year, you can use a laugh.

Low water can be discouraging, but high water is downright dangerous. The funniest times seem to be those occasions when we almost drowned after being swept off our feet in rough water. Or so it seems in the telling and retelling. Better to spend high-water time casting into a saucer on your lawn. Or have the afore-mentioned bimbo wade on ahead of you, unless you can wade like our expert here.

Getting caught by the game warden (do they really call them "conservation officers" nowadays?) is a fear, real or otherwise. The one day you leave your license on the other jacket, hat, or vest, along comes the law. You're really up a tree, literally or figuratively. If you are, literally, hold onto your fly box. Or you will be a up tree. Figuratively, that is.

Here are those posters again, which allow you to trespass *only* if you . . . and then follows a list as long as your arm. Later on, about a mile upstream, you hook a fine fish. Now what was it that poster said? No kill? And was it under, or over, fourteen inches for a keeper? What's the difference? By the time you get back to your car, the landowner's had a change of heart, and a new poster reads, in big letters: NO FISHING.

Most people don't rank ice floes as every-day boogeymen, but for the early-spring angler they can create ticklish situations. If ice chunks aren't lifting your line off the bottom and dragging it downstream, they are lifting *you* off your feet and heading you in the same direction. When you begin to feel like Washington crossing the Delaware, it's time to head for shore. Washington, of course, is dead, which should tell you something about playing around with ice chunks in the river.

This is one of our favorites. You've just missed the lunker of a lifetime. He's just broken your brand new graphite nine-footer. You've just smashed your reel, net, wading staff, and creel to finish off the catastrophe. There is nothing else nearby to break so you sit down to cool off. Before you can, who comes along but Dudley Doright. "Hi, how they biting? Missed one, eh? Too bad, you try to horse it in or something? Hey, get your hands off my throat . . . !"

"The Shattering of the Calm" is what we call it. Years ago we considered talkers astream a real curse. "Shhh . . . you'll scare the fish!"
A kingfisher slamming into a pool was a real putdown of rising trout. Since then dirt bikes, horseback riders, cows, and even
four-wheelers have blasted through the streams or pools where we were stalking about. Now it's joggers, too. They seem to have
an affinity for cool water, especially during fly-fishing weather. At least the cows and horses—after crashing through—don't have
the gall to say: "Catching any?" Yeah, I'd like to catch *you* right across the . . .

The ultimate dread of *all* fishermen has to be The Little Farm Kid with the Bent Pin and the Hunk of Cord. As a further insult he will have with him a Cute Little Dog with a Crooked Ear. It doesn't matter that you are equipped with the latest graphites and gimmickry your wallet can bear. You *know* he will outfish you! At least three to one. So you loan him your rod and borrow his cane pole, bent pin and all. In minutes you have taken four nice twelve-inchers on his cheap rig. Trouble is, in that time *he's* taken a five-and-a-half-pound brownie on *your* rig. And all this while you thought you were out there having a good time.

15 Vignettes

THE FIRST GRAPHITE ROD

For the last couple of weeks I've been trying to recall one or two of my favorite fishing stories about Zendell Grutch, my turn-of-the-century hero from the Ramapo Mountains. Either my memory is slipping, or I never knew the stories in the first place, but the best I can do is to recall that Zendell was the first man I ever heard of who used a graphite fishing rod.

Now I know most of you hadn't heard of graphite rods until ten or fifteen years ago, maybe twenty if you're a know-it-all. So you'll be surprised no end as I recall Zendell and his graphite rod. It came about this way.

Zendell, as historians will recall, was the first postal rider for the U.S. mail service this side of the Kittatinny Mountains, which run diagonally eastward from the Delaware Water Gap. During those years only the telegraph, the pony express, and word of mouth were available to spread the news, and it was Zendell's job to ride from what is now the south shore of the Wanaque reservoir (which was only a trout stream then) to the railroad bed (which was only a deer trail then) just north of what is now Pompton Lakes, delivering letters and assorted little packages.

Because Zendell had to travel really light—there were still hostiles and highwaymen around looking to lighten any unwary traveler's burden—he couldn't carry a rod and reel on his postal route, so he took some twisted and tarred cotton cord, which he wrapped around the yellow pencil he used to mark "postage due" and "receiver deceased" on the letters.

As he rode his horse along the Wanaque River and Meadow Brook (just above Lake Inez, which was only a stream then), he'd unwind the cord to which was attached a homemade squirrel-tail wet fly and sort of troll it along where the trail and the stream ran together, or tarry for a cast or two in the deeper holes.

Now of course an average pencil isn't much to cast with, so Zendell had a seven-and-a-half-footer made up. It weighed just shy of seventy-four-and-one-half ounces, definitely one of your bigger rods. It had two handles (much like present-day European salmon rods), one just above the "oga" in "Ticonderoga," the other near the butt between the "No. 2" and the metal band that held the eraser on.

Now, I know you're thinking, "Oh sure, and the pencil has graphite in it so Zendell used a graphite rod." Well, that's right, and if you already knew it I'm glad I was the one to jog your memory.

If anyone has any doubts at all about this story, I have an almost exact copy of Zendell's famous graphite rod which is here on my desk, open to public scrutiny. Not the big seven-and-a-half-footer, but rather the first one he used, the smaller one.

It is yellow with the word "Ticonderoga" printed in gold on one of the flats, and farther up is the number "3" just below the metal band that holds the eraser on. Obviously, the higher number means it is a newer model than Zendell's famous number 2.

MY FAVORITE RIVER

"Each man kills the thing he loves." This is certainly true of the streams we fish, for we think only in terms of what a stream—usually our favorite trout water—provides to us.

The fisher goes on a stream to take its fish, however temporarily, and wades about crushing underwater insect life, roiling the water, creating mud paths along the streamside and perhaps leaving a bit of litter here and there, a little salt in the wound.

That the streams survive at all is a wonder, and it is only when a stream begins to die that those sensitive to the symptoms look about for the cause, and the cure. But the cure can only be the absence of the cause, and we fishers are not ready for this. Besides, it is mankind's plan to use all that is about us, even abuse it under the rationale of the word "utilize."

It is usually with these thoughts in mind that I approach the Paulins Kill, my favorite water, which I consider an intimate and beautiful friend, but one which is limping quite badly.

The Kill's waters never run quite clear. The banks are slightly tarnished with the rot of a throwaway society. Decades of pollution have altered the Kill's bed, coating it with a slippery residue not unlike brown tomato sauce.

Still, through the miracle of survival, the Kill goes on to the Delaware River and then to the sea, and will continue long after you and I are gone.

Always giving, the waters still flourish with insect life, fish life, and the animals that come to drink. And the fisher to fish.

One recent Monday evening I invited David Mann, international writer and lyricist, to the stretch above Marksboro for an evening mayfly hatch and the resulting rise of trout.

Walking up the old railroad bed to a flat run of water, I intended to show him a Baltimore Oriole hanging like a miniature colorful Jesus, dead in a tangle of monofilament line discarded by an ignorant fisher—a spider web of death knotted to twigs. The bird was at eye level and difficult to miss. It was gone—someone had mercifully cut the bright bird down, and with it the line the Oriole had meant to mend its nest.

David caught no trout. It was his first trip to the Kill. I took four a quarter mile above him although he is the more expert fisher. But of course I have the edge because the Kill is an old friend of mine. The river and I are both scarred a little; the years have been kind to us but not really gentle. Still we both survive.

We take care of each other in a meaningful way. The Kill gives me peace, and occasionally a trout. I pick up a piece of litter now and then. It's a passing acquaintance—the Kill is thousands of years old. My life is more limited but that much better because the Kill is part of it.

REELS I'VE MET

Reels are as important to fishing as, well, rods and fishermen. So much emphasis has been put on rods lately, with the advent of graphite, that reels have taken a back seat.

When an angler says "I picked up a new graphite the other day," you know he means a rod. If he says "I built a neat little piece of fishing equipment over the winter," you know he means a rod, or maybe a boat. But not a reel. No.

I admit to a certain fascination with reels, especially bait-casting reels. Maybe I just like to turn handles, or watch level winds wend their way back and forth. The flash of a silver spool revolving smoothly has been known to mesmerize me, and the feel of finely tuned spiral gears meshing can make my day.

But what I like best about bait-casting reels is the memory of the ones I've met, the ones I grew up with. I've known many from the very early hard rubber, German silver jobs to the World War II clunkers, and the lightweights that emerged during the 1940s and 1950s when I began fishing seriously.

We didn't have the sophisticated dreams that are on the market today, reels that do everything so well it's almost boring. "So, how was fishing today?" "Oh fine, I made 739 perfect casts." So what, who cares?

I'm talking about those old babies that ground, shrieked, chattered, back-lashed, and jammed their way into our hearts, the ones that did everything just short of committing suicide right there in our hands. That's the way we remember our early driving experiences—we don't recall the smooth rides. No, it's "when Eddie and I went right between the poles in that old Chevy, rolled twice, flipped eighty feet through the air and broke my leg in three places". . . You know what I mean. *Those* are the reels I remember. And you do too, don't you?

Most early bait-casting reels couldn't cast a six-ounce lead sinker, let alone bait. Many were single action, or had a two-to-one gear ratio. I'm not sure whether the spool went around twice to the handle's once, or vice versa. Not that it mattered, for the only way you could get your bait and sinker out beyond six feet was with the "Ferris wheel" cast. This technique called for pulling what line you intended to cast, off the reel, and laying it in loose coils on the ground. Then, with one hand rapidly whirling the sinker and hook on two or three feet of line, the way a Ferris wheel spins, you finally let it go in the general direction of the water, or the fish, depending on your skill.

The success of the cast (I admit to a twenty-five percent success ratio) depended on many factors. Was the line snarled on a rock, a weed, or a piece of tin? . . . or was it under your foot? Did you wing it too hard so it jerked back? It's not easy to execute a parachute cast with bait-casting gear, but we managed. Was the angle of release too abrupt? Once in a while the throw would go straight up. Everybody would scatter, sharing a mutual respect for a fast-falling lead weight attached to a glob of half-dead nightcrawlers.

When you did try to cast with the reel, the thumb-numbing chattering was enough to make you revert quickly to the throw. "Be sure to fill your spool up," the instructions had warned. It didn't matter. Is there a difference between a six-foot cast and a seven-foot cast? Full spools didn't help much. Besides, when you buy a second- or third-hand reel from some kid for a quarter, who asks for instructions? "Sure, Tommy, instructions. You want them in French or English?" These reels were actually well made and are now valuable collectors' items.

With the advent of World War II, the "cheapie" reels showed up. Enterprising and inept manufacturers combined old designs with assembly line procedures, and what came off those lines were "cheapies"—horribly designed contraptions, grotesque in appearance. They could cast, after a fashion, but badly. That's when I learned the true meaning of the word *screech*. Up to then my experiences with screeches had been owls at night, and once when I threw a nightcrawler at Isabel. But these reels, even though they had multiplying gears, would dry up internally after a half hour's fishing on a hot day, and then commence making the God-awfullest noises. Forget sneaking into the town reservoir, or the church pond. Radar wasn't needed to locate you.

Petey, the most sophisticated of my friends, knew it was the shaft ends. "Put some oil on your *shaft ends*," he'd intone. "Or some grease, if you've got it." But it was to no avail. For the longest time I believed screeches were built in, much as clicks and drags were.

My next reel was a "free spool." It didn't belong to me. It was my uncle's, but he let me use it often. It didn't screech. I thought I had found the *only* reel in the whole country that didn't screech. And it was *so* smooth! Trouble was, it weighed somewhere just short of two pounds. It was solid brass with a quarter-inch or so of silver plating over it. It was built to take a beating, and to give one in return. The spool alone must have gone half a pound, thus negating its free-spool advantage. By today's standards it would be a heavy-duty trolling reel.

My search for a reasonable casting reel covered about seven years, from the time I was eight to my middle teens. It didn't help that we were poor. But luckily for me I inherited my brother's paper route, so by the time I was fifteen I had acquired a Langley reel. Aluminum, one of the great discoveries coming out of the Second World War, was "harnessed." Yes, that's what the salesman had said: "We've harnessed this strong, amazingly light *wonder metal*, and built from it the finest reel . . ." It was almost true. The spool, end plates, and handles were all aluminum, beautifully anodized, and the spool was "anti-inertia"! Broadly, this meant quick to start, or slow to stop, or both. The Langley could cast a large night-crawler or a light spinner without added weight. The reel weighed in at a neat five ounces, about half what most reels weighed. It was too nice for its own good, and somebody stole it.

My friend Jimmy had a reel that sounded a lot like a trolley car that had jumped the tracks and was rolling down a cobblestone roadway. He also had a habit, when we fished at night for bass from a boat, of bouncing his topwater plug off docks, tethered boats, buoys, or whatever was handy. It worked, too, for he caught some big bass. But in the meantime we had to put up with a constant crescendo of Brrrr-CLANG-gurgle-gurgle, Brrrr-CLUNK-gurgle-gurgle, Brrrr-BONG-gurgle-gurgle, all night long. On a quiet night these sounds were magnified greatly, and more than once a lakeside resident would come down, in all probability to chase the horse off his dock.

It was in the early fifties that spinning reels, sarcastically called coffee grinders, began popping up. Perhaps "clanging up" would serve better. Remember that sound—CLANG—every time the half-bail pickup finger closed? And wasn't it always laying down loops on the spool all ready for a massive bird's nest on the next cast? The early reels ate up a line a trip, hopelessly knotting the older braided nylons and later destroying the new monofilament lines at a reckless pace. Full bails, more merciful on lines, showed up soon but still there was that nerve-shattering CLANG.

Every Wednesday morning during one trout season we'd line up along Pompton River ready to fish at 5 a.m., the legal hour after the previous day's stocking. And sure enough, about a half hour later, the Clanger would show up. His reel was noisier than all the others. He would work his way downriver along the line of fishermen, reaching between them to cast once or twice, then going to the next spot. He was not above pushing a fisherman aside. Swish-CLANG-grind-grind, swish-CLANG-grind-grind . . . Fishermen glared at him and informed him that "this spot is taken," and cussed him out. The Clanger was tough. He would meet each glare, reprimand, or outburst with a blank stare and cast his huge C.P. Swing lure across the river. Whoosh-CLANG-grind-grind . . . On downstream he would go, the clangs diminishing along with the accompanying protests and curses. He didn't show up the following year. We guessed that he deserved whatever happened to him.

That clanging sound more or less spelled the end of bait casting on many waters, especially trout streams. Yes, bait casting reels were on the way out.

Their time had come. Thankfully, however, there's been a resurgence of these reels. Now we sit in regal padded comfort on our revolving boat chairs, bait casting smoothly, perfectly, quietly, with mechanical bits of wizardry that can't backlash, *never* make noise, and last all year without greasing.

But I miss the old reels—all the screeching, grinding, clanging, and cursing at backlashes. I miss my old friend Jimmy beating docks to death on dark nights. And I miss cleaning and oiling those old reels so often that the screw heads wore out. I'll never say the old reels were better. Just that I miss them so much.

FISHERMEN: THE UNINSURABLES

As you know, insurance companies enjoy calling many of us "high risk," and we pay accordingly, generally through the nose.

They have us, in a word, by the short hairs.

Recently my friend, Lance Tightline, applied for insurance, and all went well until he casually mentioned that he is a trout fisherman.

The agent's face dropped and he immediately wrenched the papers from Lance's hand and began jamming them into his briefcase! "You didn't tell me you were a trout fisherman," he accused.

Taken aback, Lance said defensively: "What's that got to do with my auto insurance?"

"Just this," the agent shot back. "Trout fishermen are usually driving when they should be sleeping, early in the morning or long after dark after fishing the hutch."

"That's hatch," corrected Lance.

"Hutch or hatch, it doesn't matter, my company doesn't like it," retorted the agent. "And further, it's a known fact you people stand out in the rain, then sit in your cars with soaking wet clothes."

"Now, wait a minute," rejoined Lance, "that hardly has to do with auto insurance. Health insurance yes, but auto . . . ?"

"Auto precisely," countered the agent. "The water drips on the rugs and leaks into the metal floor. The metal rusts out and before you know it we have a claim for a trout fisher who's fallen through a rusted-out floor going seventy on some forsaken highway in the Catskills!"

"But how often does that happen?" asked Lance. "I've never heard of it occurring!"

"That's hardly the point," the agent replied. "That it can happen is what worries us. Besides, the surgical bill for digging all those tiny fleas out of the claimant after a bad tumble can be astronomical."

"Flies, not fleas," interjected Lance tiredly.

"That's irrelevant," dismissed the agent, "and isn't it a fact that fly fishermen have no property protection values?"

"What is that?" asked Lance.

"That, my poor fellow, is the desire to protect one's property so nothing bad happens to it," the agent answered smugly.

Lance was taken aback. "What's the sense of insuring something then? I was under the impression that insurance is protection against financial loss."

"Mr. Tightline, it's been demonstrated that a fly fisher's automobile can be completely dismantled right down to the frame when he is only a few feet away trying to match a flea to a riding trout in the middle of a hutch." Lance winced at this. "This last shows materialistic noncompliance with all our society holds to be sacred and true. And, I might add, a total disregard for my company's monetary structure." The agent rose to leave, then paused at the door. "Your problem, Mr. Tightline, appears to be not an insurance problem, but rather a psychological one. I mean, a man who stands in the middle of a river in the pouring rain, toying with his fly . . . really . . ." He left hurriedly.

"Don't worry," I told Lance when he related this story to me. "You have joined a long list of uninsurables and high risks."

"Well, that's some consolation," he replied wearily. "And who are these uninsurables?"

I began reading to him: "Anyone whose house is not solid steel, anyone who has a heated home, a home with furniture, an automobile, children, is over twenty-one, anyone who drives more than one and seven-tenths miles to work, or has a car over twenty-six horsepower or capable . . ."